T0403197

BE FAIR

by Emma Carlson Berne

Consultant: Beth Gambro
Reading Specialist, Yorkville, Illinois

BEARPORT PUBLISHING

Minneapolis, Minnesota

Teaching Tips

Before Reading

- Look at the cover of the book. Discuss the picture and the title.
- Ask readers to brainstorm a list of what they already know about fairness. What can they expect to see in this book?
- Go on a picture walk, looking through the pictures to discuss vocabulary and make predictions about the text.

During Reading

- Read for purpose. As they are reading, encourage readers to think about fairness in their own lives.
- Ask readers to look for the details of the book. What are the specific ways someone can be fair?
- If readers encounter an unknown word, ask them to look at the sounds in the word. Then, ask them to look at the rest of the page. Are there any clues to help them understand?

After Reading

- Encourage readers to pick a buddy and reread the book together.
- Ask readers to name two ways to be fair that are included in the book. Go back and find the pages that tell about these things.
- Ask readers to write or draw something they learned about being fair.

Credits:

Cover and title page, © Rafael_Wiedenmeier/iStock and © Jelena Aloskina/Shutterstock; 3, © ktaylorg/iStock; 5, © GagliardiPhotography/Shutterstock; 6, © xxmmxx/iStock; 7, © FatCamera/iStock; 8–9, © lisegagne/iStock; 10–11, © ferrantraite/iStock; 13, © monkeybusinessimages/iStock; 15, © stockfour/Shutterstock; 16–17, © J2R/iStock; 19, © SolStock/iStock; 20–21, © Rawpixel/iStock; 22TL, © PeopleImages/iStock; 22MR, © monkeybusinessimages/iStock; 22BL, © patrickheagney/iStock; 23TL, © Ja'Crispr/iStock; 23TR, © shironosov/iStock; 23BL, © PLCNSK/Shutterstock; 23BM, © Juliya Shangarey/Shutterstock; and 23BR, © Denis Kuvaev/Shutterstock.

Library of Congress Cataloging-in-Publication Data

Names: Berne, Emma Carlson, 1979- author.
Title: Be fair / by Emma Carlson Berne.
Description: Minneapolis, Minnesota : Bearport Publishing Company, [2023] |
Series: How awesome can you be? | Includes bibliographical references and index. Identifiers: LCCN 2022031733 (print) | LCCN 2022031734 (ebook) | ISBN 9798885093231 (library binding) | ISBN 9798885094450 (paperback) | ISBN 9798885095600 (ebook)
Subjects: LCSH: Fairness--Juvenile literature. | Etiquette for children and teenagers--Juvenile literature.
Classification: LCC BJ1533.F2 B495 2023 (print) | LCC BJ1533.F2 (ebook) |
DDC 179/.2--dc23/eng/20220801
LC record available at https://lccn.loc.gov/2022031733
LC ebook record available at https://lccn.loc.gov/2022031734

For more information, write to Bearport Publishing, 5357 Penn Avenue South, Minneapolis, MN 55419.

Contents

Awesome to Be Fair

You should get what you need.

And I should, too.

It is how we can all **succeed**.

Being fair is awesome!

Say succeed like
suhk-SEED

5

Being fair means everyone has a **chance**.

We can all do our best when things are fair.

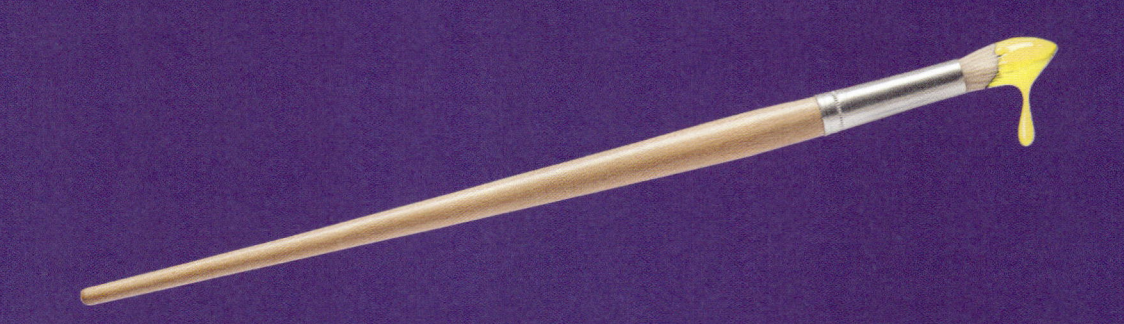

How can you give everyone a chance?

Sharing toys is awesome.

Take turns so everyone gets to have fun.

If you have lots of snacks, what is fair?

Share some with everyone.

Yum!

Following the rules means everyone gets a chance.

Raise your hand before talking in class.

Wait in line for your turn.

Sometimes, being fair means we get different things.

Fair is not always **equal**.

How can that be?

15

We are not all the same.

Everyone has different needs.

When we think of others, we can do what is best for them.

17

You may not need glasses.

But your friend might.

They should get glasses even if you do not.

That way you can both see.

19

You can be awesome.

Being fair is just one way to do it.

Let's make sure everyone has a chance!

21

Showing You Are Fair

It is fair to share the work to keep your home clean.

1. Make a list of all the **chores** to do at home.

2. Meet with your family. Talk about who will do what.

3. Switch jobs every week. Taking turns makes things fair.

Glossary

chance the possibility of doing something

chores small jobs done around the home

equal the exact same

sharing splitting up between people

succeed to have done something well

Index

Read More

Nelson, Penelope S. *Being Fair (Building Character).* Minneapolis: Jump!, Inc., 2020.

Peters, Katie. *Playing Fair (Be a Good Sport).* Minneapolis: Lerner Publications, 2022.

Learn More Online

1. Go to **www.factsurfer.com** or scan the QR code below.
2. Enter "**Be Fair**" into the search box.
3. Click on the cover of this book to see a list of websites.

About the Author

Emma Carlson Berne lives with her family in Cincinnati, Ohio. She tries to be fair, though her three sons sometimes tell her otherwise.